I0845486

PETER AND BUDDY

BY
DONNA WEBERNICK

PETER

AND

BUDDY

BY

DONNA WEBERNICK

ALL GRAPHICS WERE TAKEN
FROM CANVA AND MADE INTO MY
DESIGN

Dear Reader,

I once had a beagle named Buddy who gave us unconditional love. We loved him back.

Thank you for purchasing my book.

DONNA WEBERNICK

Mr. McGregor, the school bus driver, announced to the children that he had a puppy he wanted to give to a good family before the children had gotten off the bus.

"Would you like him, Peter?"
asked Mr. McGregor.

"Sure, I would love him,"
he replied, "but before I
commit, I need to ask my
mom first."

"Okay," said Mr. McGregor. "I'll bring the puppy over today if your mom says it's okay."

Mom permitted Mr. McGregor to bring the puppy over for her to meet before Peter asked if he could give the puppy a good home.

"Peter, this puppy is adorable! I understand how much you want to keep him but let me talk to your dad first. I promise to get back to you as soon as I can." said Mom. Mr. McGregor took the puppy home for now; he knew he needed to make the right decision for everyone involved.

When Peter's Dad came home from work, Mom told him about the puppy and how adorable he was.

Dad agreed to let Peter have the puppy as long as he takes good care of him.

"Peter, Dad said you can
have the puppy, but you
must take good care of him."

Peter eagerly asked his mom, "Can we get the puppy now?"

"Yes, Peter, we can." said Mom. That evening, Peter and his mom went to Mr. McGregor's house to pick up their new puppy.

"What will you name
him, Peter?" asked
Mom.

Peter replied. "I will name him Buddy. He is my new friend."

"Buddy and I are planning to
play outside for a while."

"We will go for walks
together."

"Buddy and I plan to
picnic at the park."

"That sounds like fun! But first, we must take Buddy to the pet store and buy him food and toys," said Mom.

Buddy selected a ball
and a bone.

"I don't know who is more excited, you or Buddy!" said Mom. "We both are," replied Peter.

They hopped into the car
and drove home. Peter was
so excited to play with his
new furry friend.

Upon arriving home, Peter and
Buddy played outside until
dinner was ready.

After dinner, Peter and Buddy were tired from playing outside. Finally, Mom said, "Peter, it is time to bathe and go to bed."

"Mom, can you read us a
book?" Peter asked. "Yes, I
will," Mom replied.

Next thing you know, they
are fast asleep.